The Whole Truth...and Other Myths

Retelling Ancient Tales

H.M. HOOVER

with commentaries by CARLA McK. BRENNER

WILLIAM JAMES WILLIAMS

Featuring works from the NATIONAL GALLERY OF ART, Washington

This book is made possible
by a grant from the
Vira I. Heinz Endowment

Project research and concept
development: Linda Downs,
Donna Mann, Barbara S. Moore,
Kathy Walsh-Piper, Anne Zapletal

Edited by Jane Sweeney
Designed by Carol Beehler
Produced by the Editors Office,
National Gallery of Art
Illustrations (pp. 26, 45, 67) by Rebecca Kingery

Second printing

Unless otherwise noted,
all works are from the
National Gallery of Art, Washington

Library of Congress Cataloging-in-Publication Data
Hoover, H.M.
The whole truth—and other myths: retelling ancient
tales / H.M. Hoover; with commentaries by Carla McK.
Brenner, William James Williams.
p.   cm.
Includes bibliographical references and index.
Summary: Retells well-known classical myths using
works of art in Washington D.C.'s National Gallery as
illustrations. Also includes information about the paintings, sculptures, and artists.
ISBN 0–89468–267–9 (pbk.)
1. Mythology, Classical—Juvenile literature.
2. Mythology, Classical, in art—Juvenile literature.
3. National Gallery of Art (U.S.)—Juvenile literature.
[1. Mythology, Classical. 2. Mythology, Classical, in art.
3. Art appreciation. 4. National Gallery of Art (U.S.)]
1. Brenner, Carla McKinney, 1951–   . 11. Williams,
William James, 1942–   . 111. Title.
BL725.H66   1996
292. 1'3–dc21   96-47313
                                            CIP
                                            AC

Cover: Detail of *The Feast of the Gods* (p. 80)
Frontispiece: Detail of *The Fall of Phaeton* (p. 34)

Contents

"The whole truth is seldom called for."

Mercury greets visitors to the National Gallery of Art in Washington. The statue represents the messenger of Jupiter, king of the gods. Mercury flew "as fleet as thought to do Jupiter's bidding," carrying the god's instructions down from Mount Olympus to humanity.

Mercury was kept so busy that he appears in more myths than any other god. Because he knew the dangers of traveling alone, it was his job to protect travelers and watch out for lonely shepherds in the hills. Many crossroads were marked by tall stones sacred to him.

A superb athlete, he was the god of boxers, wrestlers, and gymnasts. And he was the god not only of the marketplace but also of thieves.

The most startling of Mercury's duties was to guide the dead, leading souls to their final home in the Underworld. He was, in short, responsible for most things that require fast thinking, skill, and dexterity.

It was his precocious cunning as a thief that got him into trouble with Apollo, and his love of music that made them become great friends. Myths say it happened this way.

One day, when he was still very young, Mercury went out walking and soon came upon Apollo tending his herd of fine brown and white cattle. For want of anything better to do, Mercury decided to steal them.

He hid among the trees beside the meadow and waited for his chance. While he waited he stripped bark from a fallen oak log and shaped it into shoes, then gathered grass and braided it into rope. When night came and Apollo went home to eat, little Mercury slipped out of the woods, tied the bark shoes onto the cows' feet with the grass rope, and drove the herd away. When Apollo returned, all he found was a lot of shoe-prints in the dust of the road.

Apollo hunted his cattle for days. Searching in the hills, he heard beautiful music coming from a cave and decided to investigate. He was fond of music. On his way up to the cave he met a nymph and asked her, "Who is the musician playing in that cave?"

"It is a wonderful little boy! He's so clever that he made a musical instrument from a tortoise shell strung with cow gut. In fact he's just sung his mother to sleep."

While the nymph was talking Apollo noticed a brown and white cowhide drying in the sun beside the mouth of the cave.

"I think that boy stole my cattle," he said.

"That child couldn't be a cattle thief," said the nymph, indignant at the very idea. "Just listen to him play."

"All I know is that one of my cows used to wear this," said Apollo, and, rolling up the hide, carried it with him into the cave, calling, "Wake up, Maia. Your son stole my cattle!"

Like the nymph, Mercury's mother refused to believe her son was guilty. And being a god, Apollo refused to argue with her. Instead, he simply picked up Mercury and took him and the hide up to Olympus to complain to Jupiter.

"He's a baby," said Jupiter when he had heard the charge. "He couldn't have taken the cattle."

"I know he did it," insisted Apollo. "Here's the hide. And he used fresh gut to make strings for his lyre. Look at him smiling—he thinks all this is funny!"

Apollo went on complaining until Mercury grew tired of listening.

"All right. I did it. I confess," Mercury said.

Jupiter asked Mercury, "How could you have stolen those cattle?"

"It was easy," said Mercury, and, to Jupiter's amazement, told him exactly how he'd done it. Even so, Jupiter wouldn't have believed him if Apollo hadn't confirmed the detail about the shoe-prints on the road.

"Give back those cows!" thundered Jupiter.

Apollo took Mercury home again. First the child reassured his worried mother, and then fetched his tortoise-shell lyre to show Apollo, and played a song for him.

When the song ended, Apollo sighed with pleasure. "That was so beautiful," he said, "that I forgive you for taking my cattle. Suppose we go get them and let bygones be bygones."

As he walked with Apollo to the nearby cave where he'd hidden the herd, Mercury continued to play his lyre. By the time they got there, Apollo said, "Let's make a bargain. If you give me your lyre, you can keep the cows."

"Agreed," said Mercury, and that was how Apollo got his lyre.

Having been penned up for several days, the cattle were hungry. Apollo opened the gate and let them out to graze. To pass the time while the cattle ate, Mercury cut some reeds, made them into a flute, and played Apollo another song.

Again Apollo was enchanted by the music. "If you give me the flute, too, I'll give you my golden staff to herd the cows," he said. "You'll become the god of herdsmen and shepherds."

Mercury thought it over. "My flute is worth more than a gold staff," he said finally, "but if you teach me how to tell fortunes, too. . . . I suppose I could make the trade."

"I can't do that," said Apollo, "but if you visit my old nurses who live on Mount Parnassus, they will teach you."

They shook hands on the bargain. And that is how Mercury got Apollo's gold caduceus and a reputation as a crafty trader.

The pair returned to Olympus to tell Jupiter of their bargains. Jupiter had to suppress a smile when he heard that the brilliant Apollo had traded a herd of fine cattle and his golden staff for two musical toys.

"You must learn to respect the rights of property and try not to tell lies," he told Mercury, "but aside from that, you seem to be a most inventive as well as persuasive godling."

"Then make me your herald," said Mercury, "and I will be responsible for all divine property. And I will never lie, but I can't promise to tell the whole truth."

"The whole truth is seldom called for," said Jupiter.

After assigning Mercury a variety of other duties to utilize his full talents, and to keep him so busy he couldn't get in trouble, Jupiter gave him a round gold hat to protect him from the rain and winged gold sandals to speed him on his way. ■

This Mercury is the first work of art that many visitors see at the National Gallery of Art. He seems to alight in the rotunda, landing on a fountain that was created especially for him before the museum opened in 1941. To suggest that the divine messenger floats through the sky, the sculptor put him on a gust of air blowing from the mouth of a baby wind god.

But what really communicates the idea of Mercury's flight is his extravagant, active pose. He glides on tiptoe. Arms and legs fly out in all directions, while his body twists nimbly and his neck cranes upward. The bronze is polished so thoroughly that it acts like a mirror. The slightest shift in our glance makes the reflected light flicker and shimmer, setting Mercury in motion and making him seem almost weightless.

Most gods and goddesses can be identified by the things they hold or how they are dressed. **Mercury** usually carries the **snake-entwined caduceus** that Apollo gave him. And since he is a traveler, he often wears a **round hat** to protect against sun and rain, and sometimes a short cloak. His sandals or boots, or even his feet, have **wings**.

Mercury, Italian, 16th century, Andrew W. Mellon Fund

Instead of streaking through the sky, this Mercury leans quietly. His bent knee, crooked elbows, and turned head all seem designed to make an interesting silhouette from the front. The statue is finished on the back, but could just as easily stand in a niche. The rotunda Mercury, by contrast, would seem imprisoned in a small space.

Who was the sculptor?

The National Gallery's statue is a copy of a famous Mercury made in the mid 1500s by the sculptor called Giambologna. Giambologna was born in the Netherlands but moved to Florence and, after Michelangelo died, became the most important sculptor in Italy. In 1565 he was asked by the university of Bologna to create a statue of Mercury atop a pillar. The messenger god was to remind students that "wisdom comes down from heaven." Giambologna never completed this commission, but the idea inspired him to do several other statues of Mercury in flight.

Custom-ordered?

We are still not certain who actually made the National Gallery statue. It is likely to have been Francesco Righetti, a sculptor working in Rome in the late 1700s and early 1800s. He advertised large replicas of Giambologna's Mercury that could be "custom ordered." This would fit with scientific tests made on the National Gallery's bronze that suggest the statue was made in the late 1700s. The earliest written mention of it occured in 1811, when it belonged to Count Alexander Stroganoff, a Russian nobleman who lived in Rome.

Giambologna, *Medici Mercury,* mid 16th century, Museo Nazionale del Bargello, Florence

The Bargello Mercury was made by Giambologna for Florence's famous Medici family. The National Gallery's Mercury is a faithful copy of it.

"Have you seen my daughter?"

Ceres was a gentle soul. She was the goddess of the harvest and there was nothing mean about her. Her greatest joy was her beloved only daughter, Proserpina, who was even more beautiful than her mother. Ironically, it was because of her child's beauty that mother and daughter became the only two immortals to experience the grief that humans suffer. It happened this way.

Pluto, the king of the dead, left the Underworld one day to walk the earth. He was wearing his magical cap, which made him invisible. On that walk he saw Proserpina and fell in love with her. Going straight up to Olympus, he burst into Jupiter's palace.

"I want your permission to marry Proserpina," he demanded. "She's so beautiful, so fresh. I must have her. Now!"

Jupiter hesitated. He was a little afraid of his older brother, and if he said no, he would insult and anger him. If he said yes, he knew Ceres would never forgive him, for that would mean forever losing her daughter to the kingdom of the dead. And so, the king of the gods hedged. "I can't say yes," he said, "but I won't say no."

"Good," said Pluto, who understood Jupiter's reluctance to get involved, and left.

Proserpina disappeared soon after.

"Have you seen my daughter?" Ceres asked everyone on Olympus. No one had. Proserpina's friends said they'd all been picking flowers together, and then she was gone.

For the first time Ceres grieved, refusing to eat or drink. In despair, she went down to earth and wandered for days asking every mortal she met, "Have you seen my daughter?" No one had. On the tenth day she met a shepherd.

"My brothers and I were in the hills with our flocks," he explained, "when suddenly the earth moved and split open—a chasm so deep we couldn't see the bottom. We were thrown to the ground, terrified. There was a noise like the thudding of monstrous hoofbeats, and then a golden chariot appeared from nowhere, drawn by huge horses black as midnight.

"We couldn't see the driver's face, but he had his right arm tightly around a beautiful girl who was screaming. The hills echoed her pitiful cries. Before we could move to help her, horses, chariot, everything plunged straight down into that gaping chasm, and the earth closed over them."

Grateful for the shepherd's help, Ceres gave him wonderful gifts, then went to see Helius, the sun, who sees everything.

"I saw Pluto speaking with Jupiter on Olympus," Helius admitted. "Proserpina had wandered away from her friends and was admiring purple flowers, when Pluto appeared in his chariot. He grabbed her by the arm, pulled her up beside him, and raced back to his kingdom."

To Ceres' grief was added cold rage. Knowing her brothers, she understood at once what must have happened. She refused to return to Olympus and instead roamed the earth, forbidding all plants to grow and all trees to bear fruit. Soon all that lived on earth were in danger not only of famine, but also of total extinction.

A cruel year passed. Feeling forsaken by their gods, mortals slowly stopped worshipping them. Jupiter knew he must do something. Too ashamed to go see Ceres himself, he sent one Olympian after another to earth to try to charm or beg or bully her into accepting his will. She ignored them all. "Earth won't bear fruit again until I've seen my daughter," was all she would say.

Finally Jupiter realized Pluto would have to bend. He sent Mercury to tell him to return Proserpina. She was to be sent back immediately, with his messenger.

He sent another message to Ceres: "Your daughter will be returned—on the condition, of course, that she hasn't tasted any food of the dead."

Proserpina hadn't eaten since her arrival in the Underworld. She had done nothing but sit on the throne next to Pluto and cry. So Pluto had to mask his disappointment and anger when, on hearing Mercury's message, he saw her spring to her feet from joy and run to the golden chariot, eager to leave at once.

Approaching her, he said, "Try not to think badly of me. I'm a powerful king who only wanted to honor you by making you my queen. Since you're so unhappy, and your mother weeps for you, you may return to her. But it's a long trip back, and you've eaten nothing. It would please me if you ate a little something before you left." He offered her a bowl of fruit.

Excited and not thinking, Proserpina took an open pomegranate and tasted one glistening, ruby-red seed. At that, great Pluto smiled.

Mother and daughter were overjoyed to see one another again. They laughed and cried and talked all day and through the night.

"At the end he tried to be gracious," Proserpina said at last. "He begged me to eat something before I left."

"And did you?" Ceres asked, suddenly going still.

Proserpina smiled. "Just to be kind, I tasted a pomegranate seed," she said, and saw her mother go pale as death.

As heartbroken as she was angered by the trick, Ceres sent word to Jupiter that if her daughter had to go back to Pluto, not only would the earth remain barren, but she, Ceres, would never come back to Olympus.

This time Jupiter sent their mother to plead with his sister. Rhea reminded Ceres that only the dead may eat the food of the dead. After much pleading, a compromise was reached. Proserpina would spend nine months with Ceres, but because she'd tasted the food of the dead, she must return to their dark kingdom for three months of each year. During that time Ceres' grief would make the world cold and barren. When her daughter returned to the living, Ceres' joy would make earth green and fruitful again.

Now each year, when she comes back, Proserpina's joy is haunted by the memory of where she's been and where she must return. While she is always fresh and beautiful, the sight of her now strikes mortals with such awe that they fear to speak her true name and, instead, call her Spring. ▪

Watteau painted this picture as part of a set of the four seasons to decorate a dining room. And what better goddess to represent the bounty of summer than Ceres, who was responsible for the summer harvest of grain? The wheat in her hair and the curved blade of the scythe identify her.

The other characters in the painting are also symbols of summer—the summer zodiac. On one side we find the twins of Gemini; on the other side that lobsterlike crustacean is the crab of Cancer. Here too is Leo, the lion. And the fourth summer sign? Virgo, the virgin? It is Ceres herself, looking young and fresh and painted in shimmering pastel colors.

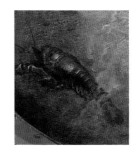

Winter, detail from a Goeblins tapestry, 1781, Widener Collection

Watteau used similar traditional symbols for the other three seasons. Spring was represented by a flower-decked goddess, fall by Bacchus, the wine god whose grapes are harvested in the autumn. He showed winter as Boreas, the cold north wind, who warms himself at a fire on this tapestry.

Antoine Watteau and rococo

About the time Louis XV became king of France, Watteau developed a charming and delicate new style we call rococo. It has sinuous curves and pastel colors, much like the seashells from which the word rococo derives. Its subjects were lighthearted and playful. Watteau had worked for a painter of theater scenes after moving to Paris from his home in Flanders. His lyrical pictures of elegant young people relaxing and flirting in lush gardens share some of the mystery of the stage, its romance, and its mingling of the real and unreal.

Shimmering colors

Ceres is an early painting by Watteau. Its rather formal design may have been provided by an older artist, but the picture already shows Watteau's own preference for bright pastel colors. These are the colors he admired in the light-filled works of artists from Venice. He was able to see these Italian paintings in Paris. One of the largest collections there was owned, in fact, by Pierre Crozat, who commissioned Ceres.

Michel Anguier, *Ceres Searching for Persephone,* 1652, Patrons' Permanent Fund

This statuette of Ceres looking for her daughter Proserpina (called Persephone by the Greeks) was part of a series depicting the gods and goddesses.

He made a golden net.

This most beautiful of all the goddesses had been forced by Juno to marry Vulcan, the homely, lame smithy of Olympus. A kind and gentle god, Vulcan never knew his beautiful wife was unfaithful until, one night, Venus stayed too long at Mars' palace. As he rose into the sky, Helius, the sun, saw them together and told Vulcan.

Angry and hurt, Vulcan planned revenge. He went down to his forge and made a golden hunting net, as sheer as gauze but quite unbreakable, which he secretly fastened to the posts and sides of his wedding bed. When Venus returned, Vulcan informed her that he would be away for a few days.

Vulcan had no more than left Olympus when Mars arrived, and he and Venus hurried happily to bed. But, when morning came they found themselves thoroughly entangled in the filmy gold net, naked and unable to escape. Vulcan appeared and called the gods and goddesses to witness this disgrace. "I won't set them free until Jupiter returns the fine gifts I gave him to let me marry Venus."

Into the room came half of the Olympians. The goddesses wouldn't enter, being embarrassed. But the gods thought it was a great joke.

"I refuse to be part of such a vulgar scene," Jupiter said. "You're a fool, Vulcan, to have made your humiliation public." He walked out in pretended disgust, ignoring the question of the valuable gifts Vulcan wanted returned.

Neptune, who had at that instant fallen in love with Venus, pretended to sympathize with Vulcan. "Since Jupiter won't cooperate," he said, "I suggest that, in return for being set free, Mars pay you the full value of the gifts in question."

"Fine, if Mars agrees," said Vulcan. "But if he defaults, you have to take his place under the net."

"Mars won't default," Neptune said, hoping Mars would, "but if he does, I'll pay his debt and marry Venus myself."

Mars agreed to pay the price. The disgraced pair was set free, whereupon Mars went home to his palace and Venus went back to the sea to renew her purity. ■

A painted poem for a bridal couple?

This may seem a strange story to choose for a wedding present. It is, after all, a story about adultery. But, for better or worse, Venus, as the goddess of love, was also the patron of marriages. And marriages, for the kind of wealthy sixteenth-century families who could afford a painting like this one, were alliances meant to produce heirs. This is something achieved through passions aroused in the volatile mix of Mars, Vulcan, and Venus. The five chubby Cupids, children of Venus, reinforce the idea.

We think this might have been a wedding present because of its strong resemblance to a famous wedding poem, an epithalamium, written to celebrate the wedding of the Roman emperor Honorius and his empress Maria in A.D. 398:

On her left stood the Graces....One pours a rich stream of nectar over Venus' head, another parts her hair with a fine ivory comb. A third standing behind...braids her tresses and orders her ringlets in due array....Nor did her face lack the mirror's verdict. While she surveys every detail and approves her beauty she notes the shadow of her son.

●n Cyprus, where the goddess of love is adorned by the Graces, velvets are rich, silks and pearls smooth and luminescent like the perfect skin of the goddess, and Cupids plump with baby fat. We are so caught up in these wonderful textures that it takes a moment to notice that in the courtyard, half hidden by the fountain, two small figures converse. These are Mars, so his arms and weapons tell us, and Vulcan, identified by the staff he leans on—rivals for Venus' affections.

Annibale Carracci

Annibale, his brother Agostino, and their cousin Lodovico established an academy in Bologna to reform painting because they believed that artistic styles had become artificial and contrived, and that their contemporaries had strayed too far from the natural world. So it is not surprising that Annibale Carracci was one of the first Italian artists to paint landscapes. This painting is among the very earliest in which the landscape itself has center stage rather than being simply a backdrop. Annibale observed nature carefully and painted it accurately, paying particular attention to all its different textures.

Annibale Carracci, *River Landscape*, about 1590, Samuel H. Kress Collection

Carracci's Venus, like this one by Titian, regards her beauty in a mirror. This is not just vanity, but a favorite image of Renaissance love poetry. Lovers expressed their envy of the mirror, which held the face of the beloved. The subject was a special favorite of Titian and his patrons. He painted at least three versions of this picture, which were copied in turn by his workshop assistants. Titian kept this original canvas for himself until he died.

Titian once wrote that he was "learning from the marvelous ancient stones." The pose of his Venus, hands crossed modestly over her breast and lap, is taken from a famous ancient statue.

Medici Venus, Roman, after a Hellenistic original of the 4th century B.C., Uffizi Gallery, Florence

Titian, *Venus with a Mirror,* about 1555, Andrew W. Mellon Collection

Venus was born of the sea foam near the island of Cyprus, so she is often seen with **shells** and **pearls**. Sometimes pearls are called the "tears of Venus." **Doves** and **swans** were her special birds, and an **apple** or **quince** was a reminder of her powers of procreation. Venus' son **Cupid** is usually nearby, and she is frequently attended by the **Three Graces**, named Splendor, Mirth, and Cheer.

Three Graces, Roman wall painting from Pompeii, 1st century A.D., Archeological Museum, Naples

"Delicious!"

Here the king of the gods is a fat baby with golden curls. The wood nymph Adrastea supports this sturdy armload as she feeds him a drink of milk from the goat nymph Amalthea, while Melissa offers the child a bit of honeycomb. While adult gods dined on the heavenly diet of nectar and ambrosia, young godlings grew plump on milk and honey. Apparently even as an infant, Jupiter had an Olympian appetite.

The goatherds double as guards, the Curetes. If the baby cried, it was their job to make enough noise to cover the sound, lest his terrible father hear and come and swallow him.

According to one of the ancient creation myths—all of which are confusing—the elder gods were the giant Titans. Among them, Mother Earth and the sky god Uranus were the first parents. Their son Cronus (Father Time) married their daughter Rhea for lack of another mate.

"Now hear me, Cronus," Uranus told his son, "I am going to die and you will take my place as king of the gods. But as you take my place, be warned; in time to come one of your sons will take your place."

Cronus didn't want to hear this. To keep his father's prophecy from coming true, he swallowed every child his wife bore him.

By the time he'd swallowed five of her babies, Rhea was quite angry. When her sixth child was due, she fled in secret to a remote mountain in Greece. There, in the darkest hour of the night, she gave birth to a son, Jupiter. Before dawn came she gave the infant to Mother Earth for safekeeping. Mother Earth took him to the island of Crete to be hidden and cared for by the daughters of Melisseus, which means "bee man," and the goat nymph Amalthea.

Rhea then went home and presented Cronus with a stone

■ **The Feeding of the Child Jupiter** (detail)

about 1640
by Nicolas Poussin
French, 1594–1665
Oil on canvas, 1.174 x 1.553 m
(46 ⅛ x 61 ⅛ in.)
Samuel H. Kress Collection

wrapped in swaddling clothes, which he promptly swallowed whole.

Well fed and well protected, Jupiter grew quickly. He spent his youth among the shepherds in the hills. When fully grown, he went to visit his mother, who was very glad to see him. He asked her to make him Cronus' cupbearer, so that he might wait on his father at the table.

"I have a plan to get even with him," he said.

"I'll help you," said she, and made him a servant in the household. His father, unaware that this son existed, suspected nothing.

Cronus was fond of a honeyed drink so sweet that it killed the taste of anything else. As cupbearer, Jupiter had the chance to slip an emetic potion that would cause vomiting into his father's drink.

"Delicious," said Cronus, when he'd taken the first sip. "Better than ever!" He continued and drank it down. Then an odd expression came over his face. All at once he swallowed. And swallowed again. And then he gave a mighty retch and up came a large stone wrapped in swaddling clothes. Another retch and all of Jupiter's older brothers and sisters, one after the other, tumbled out of Cronus' huge mouth.

First came Vesta, who would be goddess of the hearth and home; then Ceres, who would be goddess of the harvest; Juno, who would become the queen of the gods; Pluto, who would rule the Underworld; and Neptune, soon to be god of the seas. Imprisoned in the great belly of the Titan Time, they had grown to adulthood. And being gods and goddesses and thus immortal, they emerged unharmed and in good health.

They were so angry at Cronus and so grateful to Jupiter for rescuing them that they immediately asked their younger brother to lead them in a war of vengeance against their father and the Titans. Except their mother, of course. Jupiter agreed.

Atlas led the elder gods because Cronus was too old. In time the children of Cronus defeated the Titans. It was during this war that Jupiter was given his thunderbolt, Pluto his helmet of darkness, and Neptune his trident.

Together the young gods and goddesses banished the Titans to a "far western island," except Rhea and her mother, Earth. Because Atlas had led the Titans, he was punished by being forced to carry the sky on his shoulders through all eternity.

Jupiter became the new ruler of the sky and king of the gods, thus fulfilling Uranus' prediction to Cronus.

In gratitude to the goat nymph Amalthea for the milk she had unselfishly given him throughout his infancy, Jupiter set her image among the stars as Capricorn. To further honor her, he made her horn the famous cornucopia, the horn of plenty, which is always filled with whatever food its owner may desire.

Some say that Jupiter kept the stone his father vomited up. They say he took it to Delphi in Greece and it is still there. Others say that's not the same stone at all, just a large meteorite once used in rainmaking ceremonies. ■

The rational style of Poussin

The Italian sculptor Bernini once said, "Poussin works from here," and pointed to his head. Everything in this painting has a carefully thought-out purpose. Consider those reclining young women in the background for example. Visually they balance Adrastea in the foreground, the angles of their bent knees seeming to echo those of Adrastea and Jupiter.

But for Poussin, a visual purpose is not justification enough. There must also be a reason for their presence, so these reclining females are river nymphs, with a water jug and reedy plants behind them. They locate the scene on Crete, where Jupiter was hidden.

To achieve his careful designs, Poussin made many preliminary drawings and constructed shadowboxes filled with movable wax figurines. Adjusting his small models and directing beams of light from lanterns, he choreographed his paintings in the same way a theater designer positions actors, scenery, and spotlights.

Poussin peering into shadow box, adapted from O. Bätschman, *Nicolas Poussin, Dialectics of Painting* (London, 1990)

Poussin, *Self Portrait,* 1649–1650, Musée du Louvre, Paris

Nicolas Poussin

Poussin did not fully reveal his talent until he moved to Italy at the age of thirty. He admired the beauty of the Italian countryside but, even more, he was attracted to the art of Italy's Roman and Renaissance past. In Rome he was befriended by wealthy art patrons, scholars, and amateur archaeologists interested in ruins and ancient literature. With their encouragement he developed his cool, rational style.

Poussin, *Triumph of Titus,* about 1640–1645, pen and wash drawing of a Roman relief on the Arch of Titus, National Museum, Stockholm

Poussin and the French Academy

Though he returned to France only once, Poussin was accorded lofty status by the French Academy, an institution founded in 1648 to regulate the arts in France. Its rigid hierarchy put the greatest value on ancient art, Renaissance masters, and, of course, Poussin. Great themes and careful compositions were prized, not dash or splashing color. The best students were awarded prizes to study in Rome. There they learned by drawing ancient monuments, as Poussin had done.

Relief from the Arch of Titus, about 81 A.D., Rome

Illustration to Book 4 of the *Iliad,* published 1805, after designs by John Flaxman

We see **Jupiter** more often as an adult, enthroned as he is here on Mount Olympus. He usually carries a **scepter** or a **thunderbolt**. He is accompanied by an **eagle** or sometimes appears as an eagle himself.

"The gift of all."

Alone in a pastel paradise, Pandora stands absorbed by the box in her hands. In the fables of ancient Greece she is the first mortal woman. She is also the first human to have a name. Her arrival on Earth began the love-hate relationship between the gods and humans and between men and women.

Pandora's curiosity ended the all-male paradise of the Golden Age when she opened a forbidden box. Jupiter had Pandora created as an act of revenge against his cousin Prometheus who, much to Jupiter's displeasure, had created mankind from clay, modeling men after the gods. So that his men would prosper on earth, Prometheus made the season always spring with flowers blooming; the rivers ran with milk and honey, and no one ever had to work.

The only thing missing was fire, so men could cook their food and warm themselves on cool nights. Prometheus went to Jupiter, who was in charge of fire, and asked if he could have this gift for mankind.

"No," said Jupiter. "You can't. I don't like them. Men serve no purpose and I'm going to kill them."

"Please don't," said Prometheus, and begged for their lives until Jupiter relented. But he still refused to give them fire.

One day Jupiter got into an argument with some men over what part of a bull should be sacrificed to the gods and what part men would keep as food for themselves. Finally he turned to Prometheus, saying, "You made them. You find a way to settle this argument."

"Very well," agreed Prometheus. "Come back in an hour."

Left alone, Prometheus skinned the bull and made two bags out of the hide, one large and one small. Cutting up the carcass, he put all the meat into the small bag. On the top of that bag he laid the stomach, which looked quite disgusting. Into the large bag went all the bones and waste, and on top of the bag he piled huge chunks of rich fat. He knew that Jupiter not only had an Olympian appetite, but loved fat.

"As king of the gods, you get first choice," he told Jupiter when he and the men returned.

Greedy Jupiter took the biggest bag. As soon as he opened it and saw how he'd been tricked, he was furious. But he had made his choice; it was too late to change his mind.

"Just for that," he told Prometheus, "Mankind can't ever have fire. Let them eat their meat bloody raw!"

Prometheus couldn't accept that. He loved and cared for his creation and so he disobeyed. Going secretly to the sun, he stole some fire and brought it back to mankind.

When Jupiter found out, he exacted his revenge. He had Prometheus captured and taken away and chained, naked, to a pillar on a snowy mountain peak. Every day the angry Jupiter sent his huge and hungry eagle to land on Prometheus, dig in its sharp talons and tear out the Titan's liver. Every night the liver grew back, so that there was no end to Prometheus' pain and suffering. But this terrible punishment still wasn't enough to satisfy Jupiter's anger. He'd gotten even with his cousin and to get even with mankind he devised a plan.

He went to Vulcan and ordered him to make a clay woman. She was to be the most beautiful being ever created. Vulcan, a talented artisan, was successful in the task. Jupiter brought the woman to life and ordered all his family to give her gifts. He named her Pandora, "the gift of all."

The goddesses dressed her in the finest clothing. Juno taught her practical skills. Venus gave her desire and the ability to charm. Mercury gave her a lovely speaking voice and a clever mind. Apollo taught her to play and sing.

When Jupiter felt she was ready, he himself brought her down to earth. To mankind in their paradise he gave his very own special gift.

All of mankind were completely dazzled by Pandora's beauty, as Jupiter knew they would be. Still, seeing their reaction made him smile with satisfaction.

Before he left he handed Pandora a beautiful box, saying, "This is my own special gift to you. Don't ever open it." And then he hurried back to Olympus to watch his plan develop. He had filled the box with sorrow, disease, vice, violence, greed, madness, old age, death—all the ills that still plague mortals. Because Mercury had made her clever and thus curious, no sooner was Jupiter gone than Pandora opened the box. When she lifted the lid, out flew all the misery in the world. She tried to slam the lid shut but it was too late. The only thing she trapped inside was hope, which Prometheus had somehow caused to be included. Hope was the only thing he could think of to keep his creation from mass suicide.

Long afterward, when Prometheus had been freed, Jupiter denied that he had been so cruelly vindictive and, like all tyrants, told Olympian lies to excuse what he had done. And by that time, ironically, mankind no longer blamed him for the loss of paradise. They blamed Pandora. ∎

A place that is misty and serene, where light, flowers, and the air itself are indistinguishable: Redon envisioned such a world before evil. Pandora's calm consideration of the box gives no hint of the troubles it holds. It seems small, insignificant. Yet somehow we notice it right away. Partly this is because it is the darkest part of the picture.

Redon has also placed it just left of center, the spot our eye is drawn to first.

Our focus on the box is vital because it and the title are our only clues about what story Redon is telling us. Without it, Redon's picture would be plotless, like this Roman wall painting.

Spring, Roman wall painting from Stabiae, 1st century A.D., Archeological Museum, Naples

Odilon Redon

Redon lived at the same time as the impressionists. But they painted the life they saw around them—the French countryside, the bustle of Paris—while Redon painted from his imagination. He suffered a lonely childhood, shut away as an invalid much of the time. He once wrote to a friend, "The events that left their mark on me happened in days gone by, in my head."

Redon did not always paint with the lyrical mood and pastel colors of *Pandora*. In fact, he rarely used color at all until he was almost fifty years old. Before that he made mostly engravings and prints in black and white. "Noirs," he called them, from the French word for black. And it was not only their look that was dark. Their disquieting subjects, like this one dedicated to Edgar Allan Poe, seem to have come out of nightmares.

"My exquisite prodigies of light"

After his son was born, Redon started painting with color and optimism. Some of his latest and best-known paintings are of flowers, which he called "my exquisite prodigies of light." In *Pandora*, a riot of reds, blues, and greens at the bottom of the canvas start out as flowers but they dissolve into pure paint, floating up as if disembodied into the sky.

Redon, *The Eye Like a Strange Balloon Mounts Toward Infinity*, 1882, Museum of Modern Art, New York

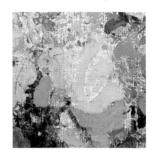

Redon, *Flowers in a Vase,* about 1910, Ailsa Mellon Bruce Collection

Redon, *Saint Sebastian,* 1910/1912, Chester Dale Collection

Around 1910, a patron asked Redon to paint a folding screen. He seems to have liked the narrow vertical shape because he did a group of pictures, all of the same size, including *Pandora* and this *Saint Sebastian.* The only thing that connects the two is their shape. They were never part of a screen, and Redon insisted that they were independent— though, of course, Sebastian was the patron saint of plague victims, victims, that is, of one of the most deadly gifts in Pandora's box.

"Anything...but this."

If pride and stupidity had not been released from Pandora's box, poor mortal Phaeton would never have taken such a fall.

Homeric hymns sang of Helius, the sun, who drove his four-horse chariot across the sky each day. They said he rose from a glorious palace in the east and flew to another palace in the west. There he let his horses graze on the Isles of the Blessed.

Each night, with his team and chariot, he boarded a golden ferry. There he slept while the ship sailed him home on the ocean stream flowing around the world.

The Roman poet Ovid told the story of Phaeton. The palace of the sun is so bright, said Ovid, so full of shiny gold and sparkling jewels, that it is blinding. Few mortals could endure being there.

Yet one day a mortal boy walked into that brilliance. Shielding his eyes with his hands, he started to approach the sun god's throne but stopped, unable to bear that light.

Looking down with kindness, Helius removed his blazing crown so that the boy could see and asked, "What brings you here?"

"I'm Phaeton and I must know if you are truly my father," the boy said bluntly. "Mother said you were, but no one believes me. Mother said I should come and ask you."

Helius smiled down at him and said, "What your mother told you was true. And I will give you proof. Ask me for anything you want and it's yours."

Phaeton had often dreamed of a moment such as this. He knew exactly what he wanted. "I want to take your place, Father. I want to drive your chariot, just for one day."

Too late Helius realized he'd made a terrible mistake by swearing to give this callow boy anything he wished.

"You are mortal, like your mother," Helius said, trying to talk Phaeton out of his foolish request. "No mortal has the strength to drive my chariot. No other god does. I'm the only god strong enough for the job. Please try to understand. I'll give you anything else you ask for."

"I want to drive your chariot," said Phaeton stubbornly. "The road rises from behind the sea and stretches up to the top of the heavens, so high that even I am afraid to look down," said Helius. "And the trip coming down in the west is worse than going up. I'm always afraid I'll lose control and crash into the sea."

"I want to drive your chariot," Phaeton insisted, and nothing his father could say could talk him out of it.

"I can give you the world," Helius said at last. "Anything you ask for but this. And if you think I don't love you, my son, then why am I so afraid for you?"

But the boy wouldn't listen. All he could think of was that he, Phaeton, would get to drive horses so powerful that even Jupiter was afraid of them. And all the world would know he was the son of the sun!

Helius talked and talked, and finally, sadly, gave up, seeing that the boy could not be persuaded. Besides, dawn was near, the sky was growing purple, the stars were going to bed.

Phaeton paid no attention to any of the dangers his father mentioned. He didn't want to listen. He wasn't afraid at all. When the seasons, the gatekeepers of Olympus, opened the gates, he saw the horses and chariot waiting. With a whoop of joy he ran and jumped into the chariot. The horses leaped away.

The first few moments in the air were as wonderful as he'd dreamed they would be. The team raced through a cloudbank over the ocean and leaped up into clear sky. He caught a last glimpse of the morning star as he rode to the top of heaven. For one brief glorious moment he felt he was truly the lord of the sky.

In the next moment he knew true terror. The horses began to fly so fast that the chariot whipped from side to side. Phaeton could barely stay on his feet. Feeling his puny grip on the reins, the team knew this weak mortal wasn't their master; they didn't have to obey him. They were in control. Leaving the route they had always followed, the horses went where they pleased, right and left, up and down, always faster and faster. Phaeton was limp with fear.

The chariot of the sun reached the top of the sky and plunged swiftly down. It came so close to the earth that the scorch marks created the deserts. Not only forests blazed, but mountainsides too burst into flame; rivers turned to steam.

Mother Earth, fearing she would be destroyed, cried out to the gods for help. The gods looked down from Olympus and saw the plight of earth. Jupiter threw his thunderbolt. The lightning struck Phaeton dead, splintered the sun's chariot, and killed the maddened horses. They dropped into the sea.

Phaeton fell to earth like a shooting star, landing in the remote river Eridanus. When his body cooled, river nymphs recovered it. Tenderly they washed off the cinders and wrapped him in fine cloth. That done, they buried him and wept over his tomb. ∎

The story of Phaeton's ill-fated ride served many purposes for ancient audiences. It warned of the consequences of youthful rashness and it explained the origin of deserts and amber. For Rubens, it provided an excuse to demonstrate his powers of invention.

Jupiter's devastating thunderbolt streaks from the right with blinding light, illuminating a chaotic explosion of plummeting bodies and horses. Butterfly-winged figures personify the hours and seasons, and their distress shows how the regular motion of the heavens, symbolized by the spoked wheel of the zodiac at the upper left, is threatened. There is not one interlude of calm, no stable space where our eye can rest; every figure, every line is in motion, twisting, thrusting out diagonally.

The strong contrast between light and dark throws the action into high relief. Rubens used color and light as well as action to create drama. Even the way he put paint on the canvas, in bold strokes, is charged with energy.

Sir Peter Paul Rubens

Rubens was one of those charmed individuals: talented, smart, handsome too. He was a scholar and linguist as well as an artist. He sometimes undertook diplomatic missions while working on portrait commissions at the various courts of Europe and was knighted by English king, Charles I. At home in Antwerp, he woke each day before dawn, rode horses for morning exercise, and attended mass before returning to the studio to paint. He was the most sought-after artist in northern Europe in his day. From his large studio came seemingly endless works of art, not just paintings but engraved prints, tapestry designs, book illustrations, and decorations for parades and festivals.

Rubens, *Self Portrait with Isabella Brant*, painted after their marriage in 1609, Alte Pinakothek, Munich

Giovanni Desiderio Bernardi, *Fall of Phaeton,* 1533 or after, Samuel H. Kress Collection

This bronze plaquette was made about seventy years before Rubens painted *The Fall of Phaeton*. Bernardi based it on a famous design by Michelangelo. While Rubens was interested in the action, this scene shows the aftermath of the events. When Phaeton's body fell to earth it landed in the river Eridanus, personified by Bernardi as an old man in rippling water. The nymphs who found his body were turned by their grief into trees—you can just see their arms sprouting branches. Their tears fell as amber, the fossilized resin of trees.

Rubens, drawing of horsemen from Leonardo da Vinci's *The Battle of Anghiari,* pen, ink and chalk, Musée du Louvre, Paris

Rubens painted *The Fall of Phaeton* while he was studying in Italy. He had drawn a famous battle scene painted by Leonardo da Vinci and used some of the horses in it as models for his own painting.

"Why don't we have a contest…?"

The myth behind this painting illustrates again, as with poor Phaeton, how fatal pride can be. This time the victim of a god's wrath was Marsyas.

One day Minerva made a flute and played it at a banquet of the gods. It was a good flute, and her music seemed to delight everyone but Juno and Venus. They kept bursting into giggles while she played, but tried to hide their mirth behind their hands. They were obviously laughing at her, but she couldn't imagine why.

As soon as she'd finished playing, Minerva left the party and walked into the woods alone. Coming upon a pool of still water, she sat down beside it and, seeing her reflection in the water, began to play. She saw at once why Juno and Venus had laughed: when she played her cheeks puffed out and turned blue, and her gray eyes bulged a bit from the effort.

Humiliated and angry at the thought of looking ridiculous in public, and especially in front of the two most beautiful goddesses on Olympus, she threw the flute away, saying, "A curse on anyone who picks up the wretched thing!" Thus she doomed Marsyas.

Marsyas was a satyr—half man, half goat. He stumbled over Minerva's flute while walking in the same woods. Picking it up, he looked it over and then put it to his lips. As he did so, the flute began to play beautiful music all by itself, magically inspired by the memory of Minerva's supernatural talent.

Thinking he had found a good thing, Marsyas walked far and wide over the countryside, delighting all the peasants with his music while they showered him with compliments. "Apollo himself couldn't

■ **Apollo and Marsyas** (detail)

about 1540
by Michelangelo Anselmi
Italian, 1491 or 1492–1554/1556
Oil on panel, .559 x 1.170 m
(22 x 46 ¹/₈ in.)
Samuel H. Kress Collection

make better music," the peasants often said, "even with his lyre."

Within weeks Apollo heard of this rival to his musical fame and he was not pleased. In fact, he was furious. And jealous. He went looking for Marsyas and soon found him. "I hear you think you're as good a musician as I am," he began pleasantly enough.

Marsyas didn't deny it, although he knew he was talking to a god.

"Why don't we have a contest to see who is the best?" Apollo asked. "You on the flute and I on my lyre. The nine Muses will serve as our judges. We'll abide by their decision. Agreed?"

"Agreed," Marsyas said, feeling confident.

"One more thing," added Apollo. "The winner gets to inflict the punishment of his choice on the loser."

Marsyas frowned, not quite liking the tone of that, but with the peasants' applause still ringing in his ears, he agreed to Apollo's terms.

The Muses were gathered, the contest began. Both of the musicians seemed equally talented.

"We really can't decide," said the Muses. "We're charmed by both instruments."

At that, proud Apollo's face flushed. The very chance that he might lose a musical contest, and to a mere satyr, was unacceptable to him. "Very well, satyr," he said. "I challenge you to do with your instrument what I can do with mine. Turn it upside down, and play and sing at the same time." Of course this was impossible to do with a flute, and Marsyas could not meet the challenge. But one does not question the unfairness of a god's demands.

With a little smile of triumph Apollo reversed his lyre and played and sang wonderful hymns of praise to the gods of Olympus. The Muses had no choice but to name him the winner.

"And now," said Apollo to Marsyas, "I get to inflict my punishment of choice. For daring to say you're as good a musician as I, the god Apollo, I will flay you alive."

And he did, bracing himself with one foot against a tree.

Apollo, the god of light, of healing, of science—who later had "Know thyself" and "Nothing in excess" inscribed on his temple at Delphi—cold-bloodedly flayed Marsyas and nailed his skin to a tree to dry. One can only assume the original source of this myth to be very old. Flaying, a savage method of execution, consisted of cutting the skin from the living victim's body with a very sharp blade. Mercifully, the victim died of shock long before the process was complete.

The moral of this story seems to be: "If you've got it, don't flaunt it in front of a god." ■

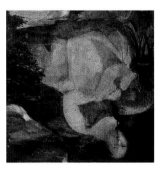

Anselmi tells his story the way a comic strip artist does, one scene after another. He starts at the right, where Minerva peers at her reflection while she plays, not a flute, but bagpipes. In the center Marsyas, now holding the same pipes, looks on as Apollo plays a violin. Finally, at the left, the god braces his leg to give greater force to his knife. Only a trickle of blood can be seen, but that is partly because a picture restorer later painted over some of the more gory detail.

Marsyas was a satyr, so only half human. His goat half was subject to the basest emotions, and not just pride either. His face is weathered and rough. Even his instrument has something a little uncouth about it, since it puffs out the face in an ungainly way. Apollo, god of reason and light, on the other hand, is bright, buoyant. The music from his instrument, we can be certain, has a heavenly harmony.

An early violin

It is probably not a coincidence that the story of Marsyas became popular with artists at about the same time that the *lira da braccio,* the kind of early violin Apollo is playing, began to be used as a solo instrument. The picture was undoubtedly commissioned by a family with musical interests. We do not know who they were. Maybe their family crest resembled the yellow and red diamonds on the bagpipes.

Pan and the satyrs

Satyrs were woodland creatures and followers of the wine god Bacchus. They delighted in all kinds of mischief, especially drink, revelry, and nymph-chasing. The Marsyas that Anselmi painted is more human looking than most satyrs, who often have goat legs, horns, and a tail. Pan is often associated with the satyrs, and like them can have half-goat form. He is often to be seen playing pipes made of reeds. It was Pan who surprised people in the woods and caused "pan"ic.

Rubens, *Pan Reclining,* possibly about 1610, chalk and wash drawing, Ailsa Mellon Bruce Fund

Arachne, a young woman who dared compare her own skill in spinning and weaving to Minerva's, was another who was punished for boasting to a god. It was Minerva who had invented the textile arts and given them to mankind, so Arachne never really stood a chance. Her punishment? She was transformed into a spider, made to spin webs eternally. That is why today the scientific classification for all spiders is Arachnida.

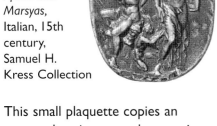

Apollo and Marsyas, Italian, 15th century, Samuel H. Kress Collection

This small plaquette copies an engraved ancient gem that was in the Medici collection in Florence. It shows Apollo triumphant.

Michelangelo Anselmi

Anselmi, a fairly obscure artist today, was not well known outside of Parma even in his lifetime. He moved there from Siena, where audiences loved warm, bright colors—like those in the red and yellow bagpipes—and the kind of decorative pattern created by Apollo's lilting silhouette. In Parma, Anselmi saw a more modern look in the work of younger artists. The rounded figure of Minerva and her atmospheric reflection in the water are probably a result of their influence.

"Father! Help me!"

Daphne, a mountain nymph, had the bad luck to attract Apollo with her beauty. As poor Marsyas discovered, attracting the attention of an Olympian god or goddess was often a fate worse than death. Or, as the poet Ovid wrote in the *Metamorphoses* long ago:

> May none of the dwellers in heaven
> Draw near to me ever.
> Such love as the high gods know,
> From whose eyes none can hide,
> May that never be mine. (!)

Apollo was on his way home after slaying a monster named Python. Carrying his huge bow and feeling especially pleased with himself, he happened to see Cupid out walking in the woods.

"Look who's there," he called, "Cupid with his little bow."

"My bow suits my needs," Cupid replied.

"And it suits you, too," said Apollo. "I can kill the most dangerous monster with my bow. You couldn't hurt a frog with that."

Angered by this insult, Cupid didn't reply. But he thought to himself: "I'll show you what I can do with my bow." When Apollo walked on, Cupid shot him with a golden love dart. Unfortunately, just at that instant, Apollo caught sight of Daphne. She was out hunting; her arms were briar-scratched, her hair windblown—and Apollo thought her the most beautiful thing he had ever seen.

Daphne, a daughter of the river god Peneus, loved to hunt. Like most hunters, the freedom of the wild attracted her more than the sport. Nothing better pleased her than being alone in the forest with her dogs or sitting on a solitary hilltop, savoring a dawn or moonrise.

Because of her beauty, many men had wished to marry her. Happy in her freedom, she refused them all, with her father's approval. Who better than a river could appreciate the joy of running free?

Then came the day when Apollo saw her and she met her doom. Suddenly aware that she was no longer alone, Daphne turned and saw him staring at her from behind the trees. Not only did his body glow, but his look was strange, his gaze far too intense. One glance and she began to run. Rape was not uncommon in the mythic world.

Daphne, a superb athlete, ran so fast that minutes passed before even a god could catch up. As he chased her Apollo called out, "Stop! Don't be afraid! I'm no rustic shepherd. I'm the Lord of Delphi and I love you."

"All the more reason to run," she said, putting on a burst of speed. She knew if he were truly a god she didn't stand a chance, but she wasn't about to give up without trying.

Apollo was so close behind that she could feel his breath on her hair when she noticed the forest was thinning. Suddenly, there in front of her stretched her father's river. From the corner of her eye she saw Apollo reaching out to grab her arm and she cried, "Help me, Father! Help me!"

Hearing her cry, seeing what was happening, and wanting to save his beloved child, Peneus quickly transformed her into a laurel tree.

Almost instantly Daphne went numb. Roots shot from her toes and her feet rooted in the riverbank. The skin on her legs changed to bark. Beautiful leaves sprouted from her fingers. Bark began to cover her hands. She was unaware when she stopped screaming.

After the beautiful nymph had become a tree, Apollo mourned, so Ovid writes in the *Metamorphoses:*

> O Fairest of maidens, you are lost to me. But at least you shall be my tree. With your leaves my victors shall wreathe their brows. You shall have your part in all my triumphs. Apollo and his laurel shall be joined together wherever songs are sung and stories told.

Which explains the ancient custom of crowning winners of athletic competitions with laurel wreaths. ■

Apollo rushes headlong up the crest of a steep hill, his cloak billowing out behind. He points to what he sees taking place in front of him, directing our attention there too. Our eyes follow along to the same point, left of center.

There, Daphne is in the very process of being transformed. She leans against an urn next to her father. Apollo's gesture and motion seem almost to propel her backward, but her left leg is already rooted to the ground. It grows now as a tree trunk, and the hair at her neck seems to be thickening into woody bark. She raises her arms, and they begin to sprout. Silhouetted against the sky, it looks at first as if she is holding small branches, but, actually, where her fingers were before, now there are leaves.

Tiepolo made his picture more dramatic with flashes of bright color, the surprise of discovering Daphne's leafy fingers, and the very fact that the action takes place not in the obvious center of the painting but off to one side.

This tapestry, on the other hand, was designed by a French court painter according to the rules of academic tradition. He included all the figures that the Latin poet Ovid mentioned in his telling of Daphne's story, diluting the action. The French Academy (see page 27) also frowned on the idea of depicting a beautiful woman with ugly bark skin, so Daphne's transformation is not nearly as graphic as in Tiepolo's painting.

Giovanni Battista Tiepolo

Tiepolo was born in Venice, a city of lagoons. He was apprenticed to a painter following the death of his father, who had been part owner of a merchant vessel. He studied with the city's leading artists and learned also from its past masters. Like Venetian artists before him, Tiepolo painted with sunlit brilliance, reveling in color and light. In his twenties he had already won an international reputation and became Venice's most important painter of his century.

It comes almost as a surprise that Tiepolo's paint is heavy and opaque, because his touch is so light. Trace the movement of his brush, following his crinkly squiggles of paint. No hard lines here, only vibrating edges that seem to emit energy like radiant light itself.

Tiepolo crowns Apollo with the laurel wreath, though this is a little ahead of the story. At this point he has not yet vowed to wear the laurel in honor of Daphne. His hopes of catching her are just now fading. By including details that are out of sequence, artists are able to point to future events.

Apollo, as the god of reason and light, is almost always a **handsome youth**, blond and graceful, crowned with **laurel**. As the god of music and poetry, he is often seen with a **lyre**. Other times he carried a **bow and arrows**. Tiepolo equips him with a quiver. Although Apollo was also the god of the healing arts, his arrows sent the plague.

Tapestry from Ovid's *Fables* series, French, 18th century, gift of Lewis Einstein

"Diana's first kiss was a curse."

Fragonard loved to paint young women or goddesses on swings. Here is Diana swinging down on the moon. She was the twin sister of Apollo and a goddess of the moon. Her love was always chaste. Still, the purity of her passions did not protect her from the pain of love.

Endymion's beauty decided his fate. When Diana first saw the young shepherd, sleeping in the shelter of a cave, she instantly loved him. Quiet as moonlight she entered the cave, lay down beside him, and gently kissed his closed eyes.

Some say Diana's first kiss was a curse, a form of death-in-life. They say she selfishly cast him into immortal sleep so that she might chastely adore him forever, as the purity of moonlight caresses the face of a sleeper.

Others say Endymion wakened after her first visit and went up to Olympus to see his father. There he asked Jupiter to make him immortal so that he might avoid the pain of growing old, of becoming unattractive to beautiful women.

During this visit Jupiter noticed Juno's interest in his young son and reminded himself that Endymion's looks made him quite irresistible—the lad was already the father of four sons by his wife and reputed to be the father of fifty other children. Jupiter granted his request for immortality, but on the condition that Endymion remain asleep. Agreeing, Endymion returned to the cave where Diana first found him and fell into an endless, dreamless sleep.

Poets say that somewhere, high in the mountains of Greece, there is a hidden cave where Endymion still sleeps. Night after night, when the moonlight silently enters that cave and kisses his face, sighs can be heard. Perhaps he sighs in his sleep, or Diana sighs with the burden of pain this endless passion brings her. Or perhaps it is only the wind. ■

Jean-Honoré Fragonard

It was said that, as a young man, Fragonard had been fired from his job with a notary because he used his pen more often for drawing than for doing the firm's business. He turned to art instead. His talent impressed some of the most famous French artists, including Boucher, who accepted him as a pupil. Fragonard adopted Boucher's delicate style and light-hearted subjects: young people enjoying games and romance in gardens, girls on swings, and pairs of mythological lovers. His popularity made him wealthy, but he outlived his own era. Fragonard was forced to flee France at the outbreak of the Revolution (1789), as the world he portrayed, like the aristocratic patrons he served, fell to the guillotine.

As Diana descends through the night on the moon's silvery crescent, its pale light washes over the sleeping shepherd. We can guess this is the first time she sees him because she pulls back in surprise, her fingers spread wide with amazement at Endymion's beauty. Cupid's arrow will certainly not be necessary here. The chubby little love god floats in on the clouds, just like child actors did in eighteenth-century stage plays, sitting on swings covered with puffs of white cloth.

Swordplay of the brush

For many years this picture was thought to be by Fragonard's illustrious teacher, François Boucher, because it is based on a tapestry design that Boucher made for Madame de Pompadour, the French king's mistress. What clues pointed to Fragonard instead? One is the strong color: brilliant blues and reds. Another is the free and sketchy motion of the brush; look at the wispy strands of Endymion's hair, for example. Some people criticized the dashed, unfinished appearance of Fragonard's painting, but for him brushwork was a part of the design and something to be admired for its own sake. One contemporary called his dazzling and quick technique "swordplay of the brush."

Fragonard, *The Swing,* probably about 1765, Samuel H. Kress Collection

Cupid

Since he appears in so many of these paintings, something more should be said about Cupid.

Once a teenager, he is the only god who grew younger and smaller with time, until he became an infant. His Greek name was Eros, but he had other names before that. Like Venus, whom the Greeks claimed was his mother, he is so old his parents are unknown. And like her, he was once very powerful. Homer called him the son of the wind and "black-winged night"; night laid a silver egg, the moon, said Homer, and when it hatched, Eros emerged and set the universe in motion. It was a way of saying "Love makes the world go round."

Cupid was never one of the Greeks' or Romans' most important gods. He stars in no myths, although he plays a cameo role in many, usually as a troublemaker. The Olympians were fond of sending him to shoot darts into mortals and make them fall passionately in love with wildly inappropriate people, often with cruel results.

We see him now on valentines, hovering over lace-trimmed red hearts, a fat blond baby with tiny angel wings, aiming a bow and arrow.

Luca Giordano, *Diana and Endymion,* about 1675/1680, gift of Joseph F. McCrindle in memory of Mr. and Mrs. J. Fuller Feder and in honor of the 50th anniversary of the National Gallery of Art

Fragonard's clients wanted rococo lightheartedness and charm. To compare the tastes of the century preceding his, just look at the dogs in this painting. Fragonard's sleepy hound is floppy eared and fluffy, but Giordano's mastiffs are guard dogs. They wear collars with metal studs to protect their throats from bites by wild animals. One even glares at us menacingly.

"Three goddesses will visit you here."

Grazing sheep, summer trees, a stretch of golden water—nothing could be more peaceful. Without knowing the story, the viewer would never guess that this meeting resulted in the lust, betrayal, jealousy, murder, and ten long years of bloodshed that was the Trojan War.

The story of the war had a simple beginning. Because the goddess Discord always caused trouble, she wasn't invited to a wedding on Olympus. Angry, and wanting revenge, she threw a golden apple marked "for the fairest" into the crowded wedding banquet hall. The guests were going to give the apple to the bride but feared offending Juno, Venus, and Minerva.

Each of these three goddesses thought the apple should be hers. After a heated argument, they asked Jupiter to decide. Jupiter knew that if he told the truth, his wife Juno would never forgive him. "You are all so beautiful," he said, "that I can't choose between you. But I know a young mortal who is extremely honest. His name is Paris, he is a shepherd, and you'll find him on Mount Ida, near Troy."

Although he did not know it, Paris was a son of Priam, the king of Troy. Warned by a seer that it was this boy's fate to cause the destruction of Troy, the king had given him away, as an infant, to a herdsman from the country. The king thought that the child could cause little harm alone in the hills with sheep or cattle.

Raised by the simple herder and his family, Paris must have been frightened to find Mercury in front of the cave he used as a shelter. Mercury said he carried a message from Jupiter and a golden apple.

"Three goddesses will visit you here," Mercury told him. "Because he has noted your honesty, almighty Jupiter wishes that you award this apple to the most beautiful goddess. They will abide by your decision."

Paris wasn't pleased with the job, fearing the gods, but he had no choice in the matter.

Now as still happens in some contests, this one wasn't entirely honest. Bribery was involved—as soon became clear once the goddesses arrived.

As queen of the gods, Juno spoke first, saying in effect, "I have the power to change your simple life. Merely say I am the most beautiful and you will become the emperor of all Europe and Asia, with such power that petitioners will approach you on their knees and all mortals will quake at the very mention of your name."

Paris thought that over. Being an emperor meant gold and glory and endless honor, but it also meant endless dull duties: making sure people had food, housing, water. He felt he wasn't qualified for such responsibility.

Minerva, goddess of wisdom and war, made the next offer. "You clearly have a good mind and the body of a warrior, Paris, but here you are, tending flocks. Give me the golden apple and I promise that not only will you become wise, but you will be victorious in every battle. You will be a hero above all other heroes."

Paris thought that over. He would like to be wise. He could see himself as a hero in armor, winning respect, glory, and adulation. Stories were told and songs were sung of heroes and their battles. But being a hero was risky. It meant leading the charge into battle and possibly getting killed. He turned to Venus.

Venus smiled and said, "You're too smart and too handsome to be wasting your time here. You deserve to be in a rich city, leading an interesting life. And you deserve to marry a woman almost as lovely as I am. Like Helen, the queen of Sparta. If she saw you I'd make her fall so deeply in love with you that she would give up her husband, her kingdom, everything. . . . And if you believe I'm the fairest, all that can be yours."

"Yes, you are the fairest!" said Paris, and handed Venus the golden apple.

Juno and Minerva went away in great anger, arm in arm, plotting together to destroy the whole Trojan race.

The Spartan queen Helen was the most beautiful woman in the world. So many princes from powerful families had wanted to marry her that her mortal father, King Tyndareus, was afraid to chose a husband for her for fear of making bitter enemies of the other suitors.

To avoid this, he had them all swear a sacred oath to go to the aid of Helen's husband if any wrong was ever done to him, whoever he might be. They all took that oath, each hoping he would be the lucky man.

The king chose Menelaus to marry Helen and made him the king of Sparta as a wedding gift.

After being given the golden apple, Venus quickly made sure that Paris reached Sparta—and that when Helen saw him, she fell as deeply in love with him as he did with her.

King Menelaus welcomed Paris as a guest in their palace. Menelaus was distracted by grief because his father had just died and noticed nothing unusual between his wife and their guest.

In ancient Greece there was a bond between guest and host; each was honor-bound to help and never harm the other. Thus, when Menelaus left for the island of Crete to attend his father's funeral, he never had a second thought about leaving their guest with his wife.

Menelaus returned to find Paris had betrayed him by kidnapping Helen and fleeing with her to Troy. Or so the king believed; the truth was that the lovesick pair had eloped. Menelaus immediately sent messengers to all of Helen's old suitors, all the kings and princes, asking them to keep their sacred oath and come to his aid in a war of vengeance against Troy. And they came. In due time a thousand ships set sail for Troy.

For reasons going back to the founding of Troy, almost all the gods and goddesses took sides in the Trojan War. But most were fickle and changed sides during the long struggle. Only three never swayed in their allegiance: Venus, Minerva, and Juno, each of whom had a very personal stake in its outcome. ■

Though they are small in the vast landscape, the figures on the left stand out because they are bright and colorful. They are almost like a picture within a picture. The three goddesses parade before Paris to offer their gifts; you can just barely see the golden apple in his lap. Paris has not yet awarded the prize.

Venus wraps a garment around her creamy flesh. Nearby, seated on a rock where she has placed her helmet and arms, Minerva begins to remove her sandal. But it is Juno with her peacock occupying center stage; we follow along Paris' arm as he points toward her. She has a majestic presence and points emphatically. This must be the moment when she offers Paris worldly power. Her red and blue costume—only she remains dressed—stands out.

Most artists depicted the climax of the story, when Paris offers the apple to the victorious Venus. So why would Claude put his emphasis on Juno instead? Probably because the man who commissioned this picture asked him to. In Claude's day the three goddesses each symbolized a different way of life. Scholarly Minerva represented the contemplative life, sexy Venus the sensual life, and Juno, queen of the gods, the active life. Claude's patron was a high-ranking officer in the French army, a counselor of state, and ambassador to Rome—an outstanding example of Juno's kind of active life.

Claude Lorrain

Claude Gellée was born in the French province of Lorraine, and as an adult was nicknamed Claude Lorrain after his birthplace. He did not live in France, however. By the time he was thirteen he had moved to Rome, reveling in the warm sunshine, rolling hills, and ancient ruins of Mediterranean Italy. Legend says he worked his way to Italy as an assistant pastry cook and took a job in the household of a landscape painter in Rome. However it happened, by his late teens Claude was apprenticed to a landscape painter and soon far surpassed him to become the most important landscape painter of the day.

Claude never returned to France but spent his entire career in Italy. It was the Italian countryside, quiet and still, that inspired him. The dark colors that frame the sides of this painting force our eyes to follow the river channel into the distance. There glows a warm, mellow light typical of Claude's pictures, which always seem to be happening at sunset or sunrise when the light is delicate. These distant colors are pastel tints of the same strong reds, yellows and blues in the figures' robes. Claude's is a timeless, perfect world, a place where gods and mortals could meet.

What's in a name?

Claude is one of the artists we usually call by his first name. This is not undue familiarity or lack of respect, but because his "last name" is invented. Many artists from early periods are called after the places of their birth, some after their fathers' first names. Others, like Raphael, Titian, and Michelangelo, have such great stature that one name is enough, even though we know what their real family names were.

Athena (Roman Minerva) on a Greek amphora, about 490–480 B.C., Antikenmuseum und Samlung Ludwig, Basel

We don't often find **Minerva** undressed or undressing, as we do in Claude's painting. Usually she is clad in her **aegis**, a cloak with a snaky hem, and with a complement of **armor**. The wise **owl** was Minerva's bird, and she is sometimes seen near an **olive tree**.

She begged him not to go.

The story of Venus and Adonis began when a proud king boasted that his daughter Smyrna was more beautiful than Venus. He thus made the innocent girl the victim of a dreadful fate. Venus, angered by this insult, caused Smyrna to fall in love with her father and climb into bed with him one dark night when he was too drunk to know what he was doing. Later, when the king learned he was the father of his own daughter's unborn child, he went wild with rage and shame. Grabbing his sword, he chased her from the palace and caught up with her on a hill.

Just as he was about to kill Smyrna, Venus, who was watching and regretting the trouble she'd caused, changed Smyrna into a myrrh tree. The king's sword blow hit the tree, splitting it in half. Out tumbled the infant Adonis, alive and well.

Adonis was such a beautiful baby that Venus fell in love with him. She promised herself that when he grew up, he would be hers. Quickly putting him in a chest to hide him from the angry king, she took the chest to Proserpina, goddess of the Underworld, and asked her to store it until she came to claim it.

After Venus left, Proserpina grew curious and opened the chest. Seeing the lovely child, she took him home and raised him in her own palace. News of this reached Venus, who hurried back to claim him. Proserpina refused to give him up. "I raised him and I'm keeping him," she insisted.

■ **Venus and Adonis** (detail)

about 1560
by Titian
Italian, about 1490–1576
Oil on canvas, 1.068 x 1.360 m
(42 x 53 1/2 in.)
Widener Collection

Venus appealed to Jupiter. Jupiter doubted the motives of both goddesses and said he wasn't going to get involved in such an unsavory affair. He sent the matter to a lower court, presided over by the muse Calliope.

In settling this custody battle, Calliope ruled that both goddesses had equal claim to Adonis, but he also should have time for himself. Therefore, she said, he would spend a third of the year with Proserpina, a third with Venus, and the rest was his to spend as he liked.

Venus disobeyed the order and cheated by quickly seducing Adonis into spending all his time with her. She was good to Adonis, doing all she could to please him.

Proserpina was justly angered by the situation. She went to her friend Mars, the god of war, who sent so many to dwell in her Underworld. Knowing that Mars and Venus had been lovers, she told him, "Have you heard? Venus has a new lover, a mere mortal. They're inseparable." Mars became jealous.

Intent on her own affairs, Venus went on loving Adonis. Then came the day when Jupiter called and she had to fly to Olympus. Having a premonition of danger for Adonis, she begged him not to go hunting without her. He went anyway.

He had no more than reached the forest when his hounds picked up a scent. The boy had no way of knowing that jealous Mars had changed himself into a huge wild boar, which his dogs tracked down and cornered.

Adonis threw his spear; the boar dodged and was only slightly wounded. The great animal wheeled and charged, knocked Adonis to the ground, and gored him to death with its tusks.

From her swan chariot high above the clouds, Venus heard Adonis' death cries. She flew down and found him, his mangled body half buried in snow red with his blood. Weeping, she gathered him into her arms. It was too late. Adonis never knew when Venus kissed him goodbye. His spirit had already gone to rejoin Proserpina in the Underworld.

In her grief Venus changed his blood in the snow to red anemones, the windflower. It is said that ever since that day anemones bloom each spring in memory of Adonis. ■

The he Greeks saw Adonis as the complete opposite of what a hero should be, and who can wonder, given the perverse circumstances of his birth. Greek heroes were strong and tough, rugged and physically active. Adonis was too interested in luxury and living the soft life with Venus. For Adonis, hunting was bound to be a disaster.

Titian's picture is based on opposites too. Right away we notice: one figure is female, the other male; one stands, the other sits; one faces us, the other turns her back; one rushes away, the other pulls him back. They are bright in a warm light, while everything around them is darkened by storm clouds. On Venus' side, the sky is lit by a rainbow, but on the side of doomed Adonis, there is a thunderbolt instead.

The bodies of Venus and Adonis are intertwined, gazes locked, a tragic irony since they will soon be separated permanently by death.

Enameled dish with *The Birth of Adonis,* attributed to Jean de Court, 16th century, Widener Collection

Titian

Titian was the most famous painter in Europe in the sixteenth century. If you judge on the basis of famous clients, he may have been the most successful painter of all time. During his long career, he worked for three Holy Roman emperors, a pope, and the kings of France and Spain, not to mention many illustrious Italian families and the Most Serene Republic of Venice, where he lived. He was one of the first artists to have a truly international reputation. Titian painted the first version of *Venus and Adonis* for Philip II of Spain. It was so popular that today thirty to forty versions of it survive, some painted by Titian, some by his workshop, and others by later copyists.

Perhaps more than any other Renaissance artist, Titian used oil paint to its greatest advantage, layering one thin, translucent layer on top of another. He painted this when he was probably about seventy or seventy-five years old. (He lied about his age to make himself seem older, so we're not sure just how old he really was.) Not surprisingly, his style changed over the years, his brushwork becoming loser and freer, shimmering with color and light.

Blooming myths

Venus turns the blood of Adonis into the windflower, the red anemone. The nymph Daphne becomes the laurel (see pages 46–51). Mythology is full of stories about the origins of flowers.

Consider Narcissus, so beautiful that everyone fell in love with him and so self-centered that he loved no one. As punishment the goddess Nemesis caused him to fall in love with his own reflection as he sat leaning over a forest pool. "Now I know what others have suffered for love of me," he cried. "Only death can make me leave that lovely face in the water." And so he died. No sooner was he dead, however, than his body disappeared. In its place bloomed a new and lovely flower, reflected by the pool. From this insufferable boy and from the flower comes the word narcissist, one in love only with himself.

Another story is that of Apollo's dear friend Hyacinthus. While throwing the discus, Apollo accidentally struck Hyacinthus in the head and killed him. Weeping bitter tears of grief, Apollo knelt by the body and cried, "Oh, if I could give my life for yours, or die with you." As he spoke, the bloodstained grass turned green again and a beautiful flower burst into life, the hyacinth. It is said that Apollo inscribed the petals with the Greek word "alas."

And there is the myth of Clytie, where, for a change, a girl falls in love with an unwilling god. Clytie loved the sun god desperately, but he didn't love her. She was so smitten that she soon did nothing but sit out in the field all day, watching him, turning her face to follow as he crossed the sky above. Soon she pined away and was changed into a sunflower. Now she and all her descendants forever turn to watch the sun.

"It's unwise to insult the gods."

Laocoön was a Trojan nobleman who was married and the father of twin sons. He was a priest of Apollo and, near the end of the Trojan War, was appointed as a priest of Neptune also.

The Trojan War had gone on for ten years by the time Laocoön enters the story. At that point, it seemed the Trojans had won. The Greeks had been unable to breach the fabled walls of Troy. Thousands had died in battle and of disease. Helen was still inside the city.

In Troy, King Priam's son and heir, Hector, was dead, killed by the great Achilles. Paris then killed Achilles, by shooting him in the heel, but was wounded in the fight and died a few days later.

With Paris dead, half the men of Troy wanted Helen. The enchantment having died with her lover, Helen now remembered that she was queen of Sparta. She asked to be returned to Menelaus. King Priam refused. One night a sentry caught her trying to climb down a rope from the top of the city wall. Captured, she was taken by force in marriage by Prince Diephobous, whom she hated.

The Greek army knew that if a way wasn't soon found to win the war, they must give up and go home. Determined not to be humiliated, they turned for help to the most cunning among them, Ulysses. With the inspiration of the goddess Minerva, he came up with a plan.

Out of sight of the Trojans, he had skilled carpenters make a hollow wooden horse so large that a group of men could hide inside it. Ulysses would be among them as their leader.

When the wooden horse was ready the men would climb inside, the Greek army would break camp, board their ships, and pretend to sail away. But instead of going home, the ships would hide behind a nearby island and wait for a signal from Troy.

"We'll leave one man behind," said Ulysses. "My cousin, Sinon. It will be his job to convince the Trojans to move the horse into Troy. At night, when the Trojans are sleeping, we'll climb down from the horse, kill the sentries, signal you with a torch from the top of the wall, and open the city gates."

His fellow Greeks accepted the plan. A night came when all was ready. They gathered their gear, loaded the ships, set fire to what they had to leave behind, and left.

The following dawn, the last day of Troy, her people woke to find the Greek army gone. Standing high among the smoldering remains of the various encampments was a giant wooden horse.

Overjoyed, the Trojans walked freely outside the city walls for the first time in ten years, exploring the deserted camp, strolling the beach. Satisfied the enemy had gone, they went up to get a closer look at the awesome wooden horse.

It was then that cousin Sinon came running out of hiding to play his part. A skilled actor, he let himself be bound and taken before King Priam, crying desperately all the way.

"I beg you, have pity on me," he sobbed to the king. "I don't want to be a Greek anymore."

Among the people on the beach was the priest Laocoön and his sons. When he'd first seen the horse that morning, he had advised King Priam to destroy it. "After so long and bloody a war," he said, "I fear the Greeks even when they bear gifts." Now, listening to Sinon, he again warned, "Don't trust him. You know he's Ulysses' cousin."

"Let him speak," ordered King Priam. "The war is over. As the victors, we can be gracious to one we defeated."

"It was my noble cousin Ulysses who wanted to kill me as a blood sacrifice to Minerva," sobbed Sinon. "Only the gods know how I escaped. I've hidden for days without food or decent water in that mosquito-ridden swamp, waiting for them to sail. I'll never see my home again!" he added, crying harder.

Priam believed him, ordered that he be untied, and asked for an explanation of the horse.

"It was an offering to Minerva," Sinon told the old king. "They deliberately made it too big to be taken into Troy—just in case you captured it. They thought that if you could get it inside and up to her temple, Minerva would look kindly on you Trojans. And of course they wanted to avoid that."

Priam said, "Of course."

When Sinon had finished his well-rehearsed story, Laocoön repeated his warning more firmly. "Don't trust Greeks bearing gifts!" he told Priam, and with that, he threw his spear into the horse's flank. The spear struck deep, the echoing thud revealing the horse was hollow.

Priam broke the awed silence that resulted. "You have desecrated a gift to Minerva," he said. "It's unwise to insult the gods—even though the gift was made by our enemies."

"You speak of insulting the gods," said Laocoön. "Don't you think we should sacrifice to Neptune, to regain his favor? We haven't honored him since you stoned his priest to death ten years ago for refusing to welcome Helen."

Priam agreed and Laocoön and his sons set to building an altar for Neptune. As they worked there was a sudden outcry. People were pointing out to sea. Two monstrous sea serpents were swimming fast toward shore, their bodies making *S*-curves across the sparkling waves. Straight up the beach they came, directly to Laocoön's sons, coiled around them tightly, and crushed them to death. Laocoön tried to save his boys, and the serpents killed him, too.

Unwrapping their loathsome coils from the crushed and bloody bodies, they glided away, past the terrified onlookers, up through the gates of Troy and into the temple of Minerva, where they vanished.

The sea serpents were sent by the gods. Some say Neptune, some say Apollo. Both felt Laocoön had offended them in the past, and the gods were often cruel. To the terrified Trojans, the sea serpents seemed to be punishment from Neptune.

King Priam immediately reconsecrated the wooden horse in Minerva's name and ordered it taken to her temple in the city, the sooner the better. And so, all together, singing and shouting with relief that the war was over, the Trojans pushed and pulled their doom into the city.

The horse was so big they had to take the gates off the huge hinges and remove some of the building stones to get it inside the walls, but they did the work gladly. They replaced the stones and rehung the gates before everyone went to an enormous banquet celebration at Priam's palace.

They went to bed that night feeling they could sleep in peace for the first time in ten years. Only Helen remained awake, listening, remembering. . . waiting.

When dawn came all that remained of Troy were the dead and a few women and children who were either killed or taken back to Greece as slaves. Total looting and sacking went on for three days and then the proud city was burned until only the stones remained.

Venus, who, in receiving the golden apple, had started all this grief, arranged for Helen to be rescued the night Troy fell.

Climbing down from the inside of the horse, Menelaus and Ulysses had raced to the palace of her new Trojan husband, who was a skilled and agile fighter. As the prince was about to kill Menelaus, Helen came down the stairs behind them and stabbed the prince to death. Menelaus realized then that she still cared for him and they went home together. ∎

El Greco

The name El Greco is a combination of Italian and Spanish for "the Greek." Domenikos Theotokopoulos was the artist's real name, and he started out as an icon painter on his native island of Crete. He went to Italy to learn western-style painting in Venice and Rome and eventually moved to Toledo. In Spain he was isolated from most of the art world. Many of the myths about him—that he was insane, that he had poor eyesight, that he was a mystic or prophet of modern art—can be explained by the simple fact that he continued to paint in a style that had gone out of fashion.

Ghostly and pale, Laocoön wrestles with the snakes sent by the gods to destroy him and his sons. The snakes seem like something out of a nightmare—unreal, unsettling. Behind them, a small horse, the Trojan Horse, trots toward the distant city. This is not Troy, however, but El Greco's own Toledo. We can recognize its walls and gates.

An enigma

Scholars have always wondered why El Greco painted this picture. As far as we know, it is the only story from myth that he ever did, and then only at the end of his life. What were his motives? He painted several copies, so it must have seemed important to him. And why did he set it in Toledo?

Mannerism

When El Greco was in Rome he saw works like this one, done in the highly artificial and intellectual style we call mannerism. But after El Greco left Italy, artists there took a new approach and tried to make their paintings look more realistic, leaving El Greco still headed in the opposite direction. In Spain El Greco continued to push mannerism to its very limits. He compressed space in unnatural ways and used bizarre colors; he made bodies impossibly long and twisted them into serpentine poses. All this gave his painting a haunting intensity.

Pontormo, *Monsignor della Casa,* probably 1541/1544, Samuel H. Kress Collection

These figures who survey the scene might provide clues, but they are unfinished (notice the extra head and limbs still visible after a figure was partially repainted) and so they only contribute to the mystery. We can't tell who they represent.

A challenge to artists

It seems El Greco was inspired by a famous work of ancient sculpture. In 1506, a marble statue of Laocoön and his sons was found buried in Rome. It was recognized as one of the most famous of all ancient works of art. The Roman writer Pliny had praised it as "surpassing anything in the arts." Among those who came to see it still in the ground was Michelangelo. He advised other artists to not attempt to imitate it. But the ancient statue was a challenge to artists. They produced countless new Laocoöns—on medals, painted in oil and fresco, sculpted in bronze and marble, even drawn in caricature.

Most copied it closely—even the painter of this earthenware dish ignored Michelangelo's advice—but El Greco took a different approach. Confronted with something so respected that it almost seemed untouchable, he rearranged it on purpose. Since the marble Laocoön is placed high, El Greco put his low. Because the statue has a strong, muscled body, El Greco's is gaunt and sinewy. And because of these things, El Greco created not some pale copy, but a powerful original all his own.

Laocoön, probably 1st century A.D., after a Hellenistic or Roman original, Vatican Museums, Vatican City

Maiolica dish with Laocoön, Italian, 16th century, Widener Collection

El Greco, *View of Toledo,* about 1600, Metropolitan Museum of Art, New York, bequest of Mrs. H.O. Havemayer

Laocoön 73

"They'd found their prey!"

This image of Diana, the huntress, represents the maiden moon goddess forever running with swiftness and lithe grace. Manship captured a hauntingly beautiful figure. The dark of the moon—Diana's dark side—is forgotten in this work.

Diana and her twin brother Apollo were children of Jupiter. Their mother Leto feared that Jupiter's wife Juno would kill her, so she fled to the island of Delos for safety. The twins were so beautiful that their father could refuse them nothing and so gave them great power.

Like her brother, Diana always went armed with bow and arrows. She drove a golden chariot, pulled by giant horned deer called hinds. With her ran her dogs: three lop-eared hounds that were a gift from Pan and seven hunting dogs from Sparta.

Mortals liked to see her as Diana of the Silver Bow, with all the elegant purity of the slender new moon. It was comforting to think that small children and baby animals were under her protection. She was called the Lady of the Wild Things, which were sacred to her, especially the deer. This explains the female red deer that pulled her chariot, but not what she did to Actaeon.

Actaeon was the grandson of Cadmus, the founder and king of Thebes. An adored only son, he was as kind as he was handsome.

One hot summer day in his early manhood, Actaeon went hunt-

■ **Diana and a Hound** (detail)

1925
by Paul Manship
American, 1885–1966
Bronze, H 1.647 m (64 7/8 in.)
Gift of Mrs. Houghton P. Metcalf

ing with his hounds. Late in the afternoon he came upon a stream babbling over moss-green rocks. Hearing a small waterfall, he walked on ahead while his thirsty dogs were drinking. To his delight, the creek tumbled into a deep pool. The water was so pure and clear that he could see fish swimming through the slanting shafts of sunlight on the sandy bottom.

As he leaned against a rock ledge to untie his sandals, thinking how good that inviting water would feel, a movement caught his eye.

Glancing across the pool, he was startled to see a naked goddess standing at the water's edge. Without realizing it, he had discovered Diana's favorite bathing place. She had just dropped her clothing, ready to step in. She was so lovely that he gasped in surprise. At the sound, she looked up and saw him.

For a long moment their eyes met; both were too shocked to speak. Her gaze turned to anger. Swiftly bending, with a graceful sweep of her hand, she threw water across the pool at him. He smiled as the cold drops splashed his skin.

She spoke then, saying, "Mortal, you will never boast to your friends that you saw me naked."

Those fervently whispered words were the last Actaeon ever heard. As the water touched him, he was changed into a magnificent stag. His body became a deer's body, his mind a deer's mind, his smell a deer's smell. And deer that he was, he smelled the hunting dogs and knew that they could smell him. For the first time in his life, Actaeon feared his own hunting dogs.

His hounds caught the stag's scent. One yelped in excitement, then another, and they all came running, refreshed and eager for the chase.

Actaeon the stag wheeled in terror and leaped away, up the slope, plunging back into the forest. He was as fine a stag as he'd been a hunter, but he had trained his hounds too well. No matter how fast he ran, how cleverly he dodged, they stayed with him, baying now with wild excitement, baying for their master to come! Hurry! They'd found their prey!

He ran until his heart was near to bursting, and then, exhausted, stumbled and fell hard upon his knees. And as his hounds were trained to do, they leapt upon him and tore out his throat.

Diana, still standing by her pool, waited until she heard the stag's anguished death scream, and then took her bath. ∎

Paul Manship

Manship was born in Saint Paul, Minnesota. After high school he studied art in New York and Philadelphia and in 1909 won a three-year fellowship in Rome. There, like so many artists before him, he encountered the art of the ancient world. But unlike Claude, or Poussin, or Titian, he was not drawn to the calm beauty of classical art. Instead he liked the energy and decorativeness of art from an earlier period. The springy lines and repeating patterns of archaic Greek art, made during the sixth and early fifth centuries B.C., provided Manship with the basis for a modern style.

Manship's sleek statues created a taste for the streamlined style of the 1920s and 1930s. Art Deco gave everything from bus stations to movie sets the uncluttered look of machines and a sense of speed.

Manship's Diana is a contrast of textures: her smooth, rounded body is offset by deeply chiseled designs in her hair and the dog's furry ruff. Geometry takes precedence over nature. The waves in her hair are neat chevrons, the perfect almonds of her eyes are matched by the perfect curve of her nose and brows. Even the fabric that streams back to emphasize her movement is not affected by gravity. It flies out from her shoulders in a perfect rhythm of regular, repeating folds.

Manship, *Actaeon*, 1925, National Museum of American Art, Smithsonian Institution, Washington

Manship designed his Diana to be seen together with this statue of Actaeon.

Artemis on a Greek vase, 5th century B.C., Metropolitan Museum of Art, New York, Rodgers Fund

Manship's Diana looks almost as if she is pressed between glass: flat and two-dimensional. Just compare her to this more three-dimensional nymph. Imagine what it would take to sketch them. For the nymph we need shading to capture her rounded forms, but for Diana we could get by with line alone. The flatness, strong silhouette, and severe forms that make her easy to draw also make Diana seem cool and remote, while the nymph, her leg licked by her devoted hound, has intimacy and charm. Lemoyne created this statue of one of Diana's nymph companions for the gardens of the French King Louis XIV's favorite hunting chateau near Versailles.

Jean-Louis Lemoyne, *A Companion of Diana,* 1724, Widener Collection

Manship did not simply copy archaic Greek art. His Diana still looks quite different from this ancient vase painting of Artemis (the Greek name for Diana). The statue is more supple and fluid, her silhouette more flowing. Another obvious difference, of course, is that Manship's Diana is nude. No Greek artist would dream of depicting Artemis naked; look at what happened to Actaeon.

Manship, *Self Portrait,* 1906–1907, National Museum of American Art, Smithsonian Institution, Washington, gift of the estate of Paul Manship

Diana was an ancient goddess with many different interests. She protected young children and animals and women in childbirth and was also connected with the **moon**. But she is best known as the goddess of the **hunt**. She is found in a short hunting costume, with **bow** and **arrows**, and accompanied by her **hounds**

Diana and Actaeon 79

"... and the god was laughed at by all."

Look closely. There's an embarrassing incident happening here. The joke is on Priapus. The story behind *The Feast of the Gods* was told by the Roman poet Ovid in a long poem that explained the mythic origins of many of the rituals and festivals celebrated in Rome. According to him, at a rustic feast of the gods, the virility god Priapus got carried away and tried to take advantage of the nymph Lotis.

The setting includes other guests who are important mythical characters. At the left is Silenus. He was a god of the woodlands, but he wears a small wine keg because he was a devoted follower of the wine god Bacchus. He always took his donkey with him because, it was said, he was usually too drunk to walk.

Next is Bacchus, the god of wine, as a little boy. He fills a crystal pitcher from the wine keg. By him sits Silvanus, an ancient forest god, wearing a wreath of pine needles on his bald head.

Mercury, the messenger of the gods, with his winged metal hat and carrying his herald's staff, leans against the keg.

Nearby is Jupiter, king of the gods. He wears a crown of oak leaves and is attended by his eagle. (When European nobility hunted for sport with raptors, only kings, modestly likening themselves to Jupiter, were allowed to use eagles. Lesser mortals had to make do with hawks or falcons.)

Jupiter is sitting next to a goddess who holds a quince, a fruit associated in the ancient world with Venus and marriage. Since Neptune is seated on the goddess' other side—the trident spear he acquired in the war with the Titans in front of him—and boldly places his hand on her thigh, she may be his wife Amphitrite.

Behind them in the shadows we see Pan, the jolly satyr son of Mercury. Pan was a wilderness god and a great player of the pipes. Probably he inherited his talent from Mercury.

Ceres, goddess of the harvest, appears near Neptune. She is wearing a wreath of wheat and helping Apollo with another sip from his silver bowl.

Apollo, the god of light, science, and the arts, is crowned with his usual wreath of laurel, his tribute to Daphne. Instead of the lyre he played in Greek and Roman days, here he's holding a stringed instrument from the Renaissance.

Now we finally get to Ovid's story. The nymph Lotis, at the right, has fallen asleep from too much wine. Priapus decides to take advantage of her. He bends over Lotis, intent on lifting her skirts, when Silenus' donkey brays and wakes her. In Ovid's words, "the startled nymph pushed Priapus away and the god was laughed at by all." ■

■ **The Feast of the Gods**

1514/1529
by Giovanni Bellini and Titian
Italian, around 1427–1516;
and 1490–1576
Oil on canvas, 1.702 x 1.880 m
(67 x 74 in.)
Widener Collection

One picture, three artists

The Feast of the Gods is one of the greatest mythological pictures from the Renaissance now in the United States. And two of the finest painters in Italy had a hand in it: Giovanni Bellini and Titian. In all, three artists worked on The Feast of the Gods over a period of fifteen years or so. They were not collaborators, working together, but painted and altered it at different times. It was painted by Giovanni Bellini and, after his death, modified by Titian, one of Bellini's former pupils. In between another artist had also made changes to it.

The person responsible for this complicated evolution was its owner, Alfonso d'Este of Ferrara. The duke was an important patron of the arts. He hired Bellini to paint The Feast of the Gods for his private study, a room called the Alabaster Chamber. Alfonso wanted a series of pictures illustrating the loves of the gods, all by the best painters of the day. Bellini was close to ninety, and The Feast of the Gods was his last great painting. The duke turned to Titian to finish the decoration for his room. Titian contributed three pictures. Alfonso's court artist, named Dosso Dossi, painted a fourth.

Bellini, woodcut from Vasari's *Lives of the Artists,* 1568

Agostino Carracci, *Titian,* 1587, engraving, Rosenwald Collection

Dosso Dossi, *Alfonso d'Este,* early 16th century, Pinacoteca Estense, Modena

When Bellini finished *The Feast of the Gods*, it probably looked something like this. (reconstruction by David Bull)

Titian, *Bacchus and Ariadne,* 1522–1523, National Gallery, London

This is one of Titian's paintings for Alfonso. Titian traveled from his home in Venice to Ferrara to make final adjustments to the paintings in place. During one of those trips, probably in 1529, he painted over most of the background of *The Feast of the Gods*. Titian wanted it to harmonize with his own paintings in the room, so he gave it a mountain with steep cliffs and a bright blue sky.

We tend to think of people in the past as more serious than ourselves, maybe even a bit humorless. Not necessarily. Ovid, the poet who described this embarrassing scene, was exiled from Rome for rude jokes and his love affair with the emperor's daughter. The Renaissance court in Ferrara was a lively place too, entertained with dance, music, and literature. No doubt Alfonso, along with all the gods, had a good laugh at this joke on Priapus.

In *The Feast of the Gods* Bacchus is an infant, as he is in this painting Bellini did some years earlier. As a nature god, Bacchus aged along with the seasons. In winter he sometimes took the form of a child, a bit like the baby who represents the New Year. It may be that this is a clue. *The Feast of the Gods* may relate to the wedding of Alfonso d'Este and Lucretia Borgia, which took place in winter.

Adult **Bacchus** is often slouching and slightly tipsy. He is usually crowned with **ivy** leaves and carries **grapes**—or the **wine** that comes from them in a barrel, goblet, or wineskin. He is frequently surrounded by twisting **vines** and is sometimes mounted on a **panther**. His companions include the nymphs and satyrs and old Silenus.

Bellini, *The Infant Bacchus,* about 1505/1510, Samuel H. Kress Collection

Giovanni Bellini

For a long time Bellini resisted requests by patrons like Alfonso to paint mythological scenes. He had spent his career painting religious subjects and portraits.

Bellini was among the most important and influential artists of his time. He came from a family of Venetian artists who taught him his craft. Bellini himself grew up to train many of Venice's most important painters of the sixteenth century, including one Tiziano Vecellio, known to speakers of English as Titian.

Bellini's brilliant colors stand out in the dress of the revelers. Pinks, blues, yellows, reds: these would all have been costly pigments. Blue, for example, was made from the semiprecious gem lapis lazuli. Alfonso's picture is literally rich in color. Bellini's fabrics seem to glint in the sunlight. He was one of the first artists in Italy to switch from tempera to oil paints. Their translucent layers trap and reflect light.

Also of Interest

The D'Aulaires' Book of Greek Myths (Doubleday, 1962).

Bernard Evslin, *Hercules* (William Morrow, 1984).

Bernard Evslin, *Jason and the Argonauts* (William Morrow, 1986).

Bernard Evslin, *Monsters of Mythology,* a series (Chelsea House Publishers, 1987–1990).

Doris Gates, *Greek Myths,* a series (Puffin, 1975).

Warwick Hatton, *The Trojan Horse* (Margaret K. McElderry Books, 1992).

Pamela Oldfield, *Tales from Ancient Greece* (Doubleday, 1988).

Rosemary Sutcliff, *Black Ships before Troy* (Delacorte Press, 1993).

Geraldine McCaughrean, *Greek Myths* (Margaret K. McElderry Books, 1992).

Anne F. Rockwell, *The One-Eyed Giant and Other Monsters from the Greek Myths* (Greenwillow Books, 1996).

Jane Yolen, *Wings* (Harcourt Brace Jovanovich, 1991).

Other books by H. M. Hoover

published by Four Winds Press
> *Children of Morrow; The Lion's Cub*; Treasures of Morrow*

published by Viking Penguin
> *The Delikon; The Rains of Eridan; The Lost Star; Return to Earth; Another Heaven, Another Earth; The Bell Tree; The Shepherd Moon; Orvis*

published by E.P. Dutton
> *The Dawn Palace*; Away Is a Strange Place to Be; Only Child; The Winds of Mars*

* works of historical fiction or mythology

Index

Primary references appear in
bold.